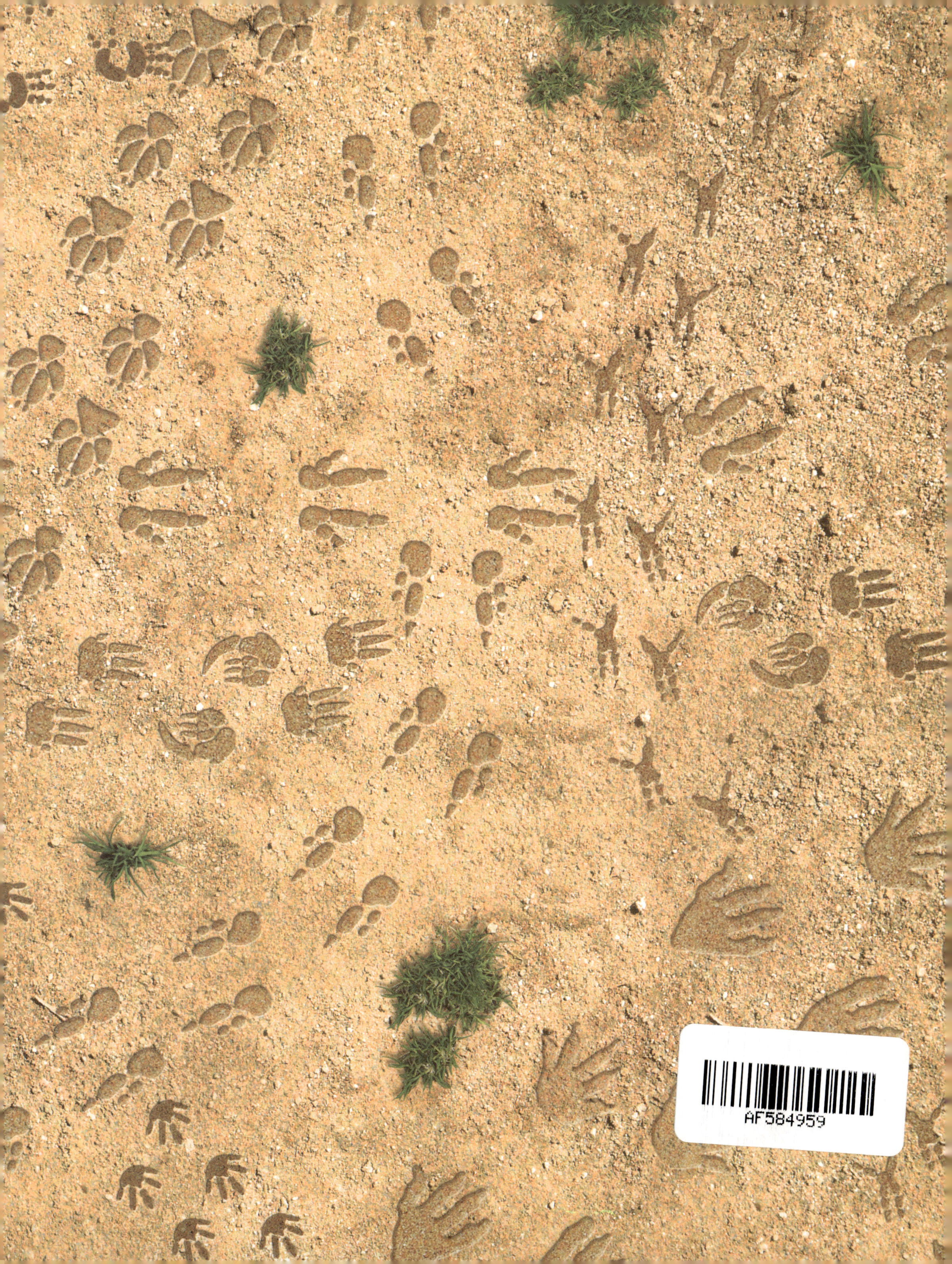

AF584959

JOHN LESLEY

AUSTRALIA'S REMARKABLE WILDLIFE

KOALA

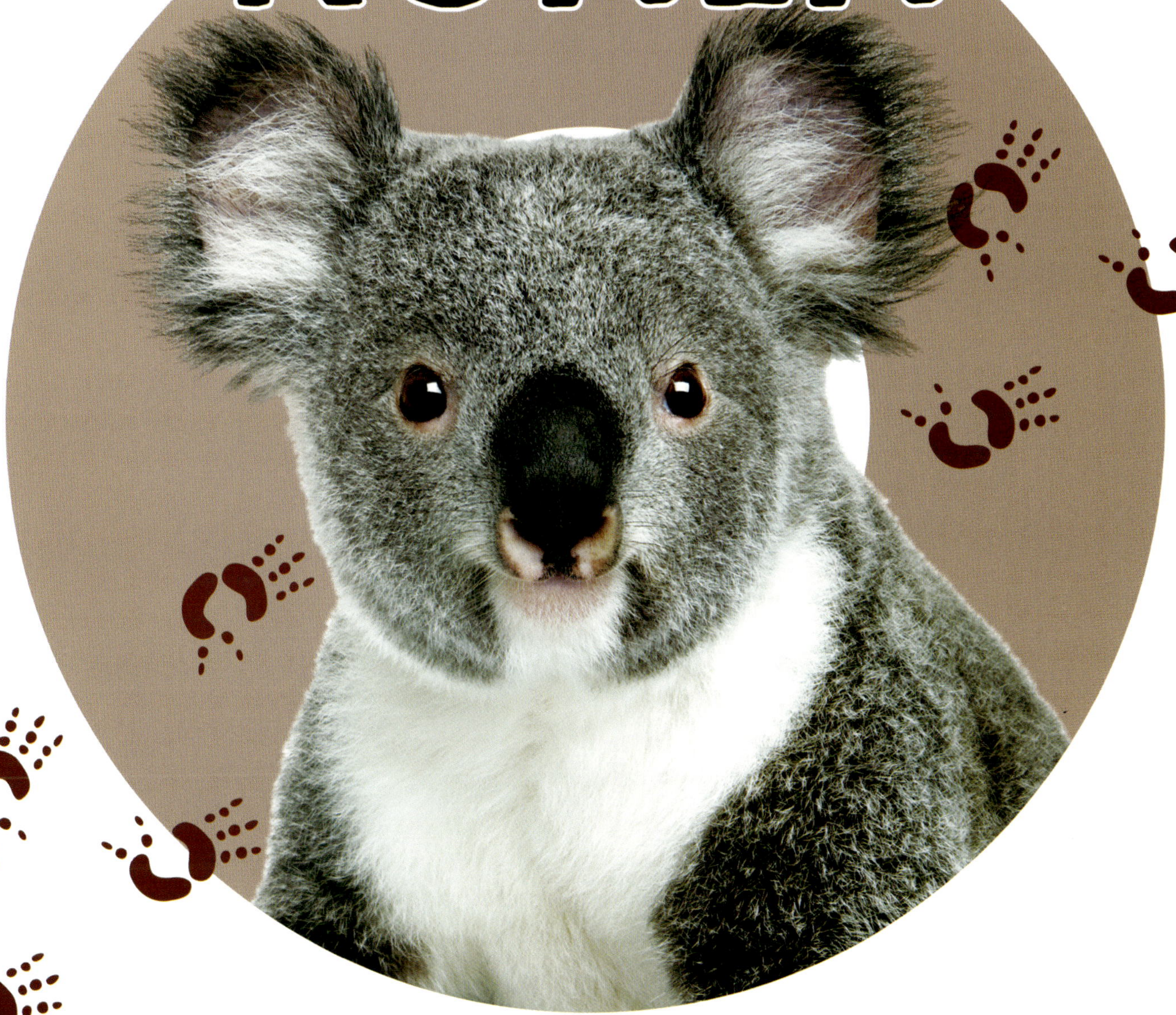

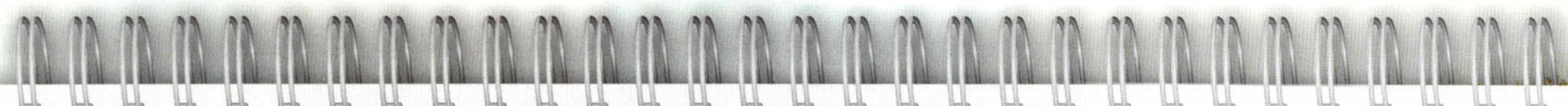

First Published 2022 by
Redback Publishing
PO Box 357 Frenchs Forest NSW 2086
Australia

www.redbackpublishing.com
orders@redbackpublishing.com

Reprinted 2024

ISBN 978-1-925860-98-6

Author: John Lesley
Editor: Caroline Thomas
Design: Redback Publishing

A catalogue record for this book is available from the National Library of Australia

Originated by Redback Publishing

Printed and bound in Malaysia

Acknowledgements
Abbreviations: l—left, r—right, b—bottom, t—top, c—centre, m—middle
We would like to thank the following for permission to reproduce photographs: (Images © shutterstock) p8tc Cliff from I now live in Arlington, VA (Outside Washington DC), USA via Wikimedia Commons, p19bl James Kirkikis.

CONTENTS

KOALA BASIC FACTS

SCIENTIFIC NAME
Phascolarctos cinereus. These Latin words mean 'grey bear with a pouch'.

TYPE OF ANIMAL
Marsupial mammal

SIZE
Males are larger than females and can range in weight from 4-13 kilograms. They grow to a bit less than a metre long.

HABITAT
Eucalyptus forests

CONSERVATION STATUS
In 2022, koalas became an endangered species in some parts of Australia.

IS A KOALA A BEAR?

No! The koala looks a bit like a bear but it is not related to the bears that live in other countries. The koala's closest relative is the wombat.

WHERE KOALAS LIVE

HABITAT

Koalas spend their lives in eucalyptus forests. People who live near forests will sometimes see a koala crossing a road, trying to get to trees on the other side. Apart from rare moments like this, koalas feel much safer up high amongst the leaves.

They sleep while safely nestled into the fork of tree branches, or spread along a branch with their limbs hanging over the side.

Eucalyptus trees are vital to the survival of koalas. These trees provide them with food and safety. Without a forest of eucalyptus trees to choose from, koalas cannot survive in the wild.

Koala crossing the road

Koala sleeping in the fork of a tree

Koalas live in forests in the eastern regions of Australia, in New South Wales, Victoria, Queensland and South Australia. There are no koalas in Tasmania.
Koala distribution
KOALAS ARE UNIQUE TO AUSTRALIA

FOSSILS

Koalas and their ancestors have lived in Australia for millions of years. They may have evolved in the rainforests that once covered most of Australia, but koalas do not live in rainforests today.

Koala skeleton

WHERE DID KOALAS COME FROM?

Koalas and wombats share a common, ancient ancestor. Look closely and you will see they do both look a little alike.

Fossils of koalas dating from 25 million years ago reveal that koalas were living in Australia when the climate was very different. At that time, the wetter and warmer weather led to lush growth of plants and trees. Over the years, Australia has become much drier, and koalas have evolved to live in forests where their ancestors would not have been able to survive.

Wombats look a little bit like koalas

THE KOALA'S BODY: ADAPTATIONS

TEETH

A koala has two sharp teeth at the front of its mouth to rip leaves from trees.

TAIL

Koalas do not have tails.

CLAWS

Their strong claws enable koalas to climb trees.

NOSE

Koalas have a good sense of smell, which allows them to pick the right sorts of leaves to eat. Watch a koala at a zoo and you will see that it sniffs leaves before eating them, making sure they are the right ones.

EARS

Koala ears are covered in fluffy fur.

FINGERPRINTS

Surprisingly, koalas have fingerprints, just like humans do.

FUR

Koala fur can be grey or grey-brown, with a white patch on the chest. Koalas in the south of Australia have thicker fur than those in the north, where the climate is warmer.

REPRODUCTION AND LIFE CYCLE

A mother koala can produce a new baby every one or two years. A baby koala is born as a tiny, underdeveloped little creature that only weighs about one gram.

It has no fur and cannot see, but has a good sense of smell. It climbs across the mother koala's fur until it reaches her pouch.

In the pouch, the baby feeds on milk and grows until it is ready to come out into the world. It then travels around on its mother's back, or clings to the fur on her front. The baby stays with its mother for about a year.

If you hear a koala making a growling sound at night, it will be a male making sure all the other koalas know that he is there.

A koala joey clings to its mother

A BABY KOALA IS CALLED A JOEY.

In zoos, koalas can live to be about twenty years old. In the wild, a healthy koala may live only half this amount of time.

In the wild, young koalas have to move away from their mothers to find their own patch of trees to live amongst. Once they find a suitable area, and if they are not under stress, they may decide to stay there for a lifetime.

FOOD

Koalas do not eat anything except leaves, mostly from eucalyptus trees. They do not usually drink water, except in extreme conditions of drought or after bushfires.

The young joey drinks its mother's milk inside her pouch until it is about six months old. A little later, it starts to eat a special form of koala droppings called pap, which is a green eucalyptus jelly excreted by the mother koala. Pap contains the bacteria the baby koala needs to help it digest eucalyptus leaves. Without access to these bacteria, the baby koala will not be healthy.

Koalas do not prey on any other animals, but they are very likely to be attacked by dogs and large cats. The joeys can be taken by birds of prey.

A young joey drinks its mother's milk before it starts eating leaves

Koalas only eat eucalyptus leaves
Koalas do not usually need to drink water

WHY ARE KOALAS SO SLEEPY?

Sleeping koala

Biologists have tried to understand why koalas always seem to be so sleepy. They have concluded that there are a number of reasons.

Koalas have a very simple diet of eucalyptus leaves that take a long time to digest. To survive, koalas have to keep on eating and digesting, and have very little time to do anything else. The leaves may also contain chemicals that make koalas sleepy.

Koalas are nocturnal, which means they are most active at night and sleep during the day.

KOALAS IN ZOOS

Most people will only ever see a koala in a zoo.

Since koalas rely on a diet of fresh eucalyptus leaves, zoos need to have access to eucalyptus trees if they are to keep their koalas healthy.

The San Diego Zoo in the USA has a very successful breeding program for its koalas, and the largest number in any zoo outside Australia.

Some Australian states have laws that do not allow zoo visitors to hold koalas. This protects the koalas from the stress caused by strangers handling them.

Zoologist feeding a koala, San Diego, USA

Koala being carried

PEOPLE AND KOALAS

We love to look at and get close to a furry koala, but humans are their main threat. Even though we do not want to harm them, people are causing a decline in their numbers by clearing forests where koalas live.

KOALAS NEAR HOUSES

Being near humans, dogs and cats causes koalas to become stressed and can make them ill. Koalas found near houses may be trapped in the last remaining forest in that area.

KOALAS AS PETS?

It is illegal to keep a koala as a pet. Any koala taken from the wild will probably get sick from stress, illness and incorrect food. Zoos, wildlife carers and some scientists are allowed to keep koalas under very strict conditions.

A koala with a wildlife carer

ARE DROP BEARS REAL?

Have you heard people claiming to have been attacked by a drop bear? Drop bears are an Aussie fable. Don't tell anyone the truth though - that would spoil the fun!

ARE KOALAS DANGEROUS?

Koalas look cuddly and calm, but they have very strong claws and large front teeth. Big male koalas, or a female with a baby, can become aggressive if they feel that people are a threat to them.

THINK ABOUT HABITATS

People need places to live and work, and this is why forests are disappearing. Think about ways that koalas and people can both have the homes that they want. The more we discuss the possibilities, the more likely we are to find a solution to the problem.

HOW TO HELP INJURED KOALAS

If you find an injured koala by the side of a road, you will want to help it in some way. Here are some things you can do:

Get adult help before assisting any injured animal on or near a road, or you may get injured too.

If the koala is alive, ring a wildlife carer. The koala will be very frightened and may scratch or bite.

If the koala is dead, check if a live joey is in the pouch. If you find one, do not remove it but take the dead animal with the joey in its pouch to a place that knows how to help.

Avoid offering food or drink. The wrong type of liquids can kill a joey.

It is illegal to keep a koala.

A sick koala needs expert attention, so do not take it home.

NEXT 2 km

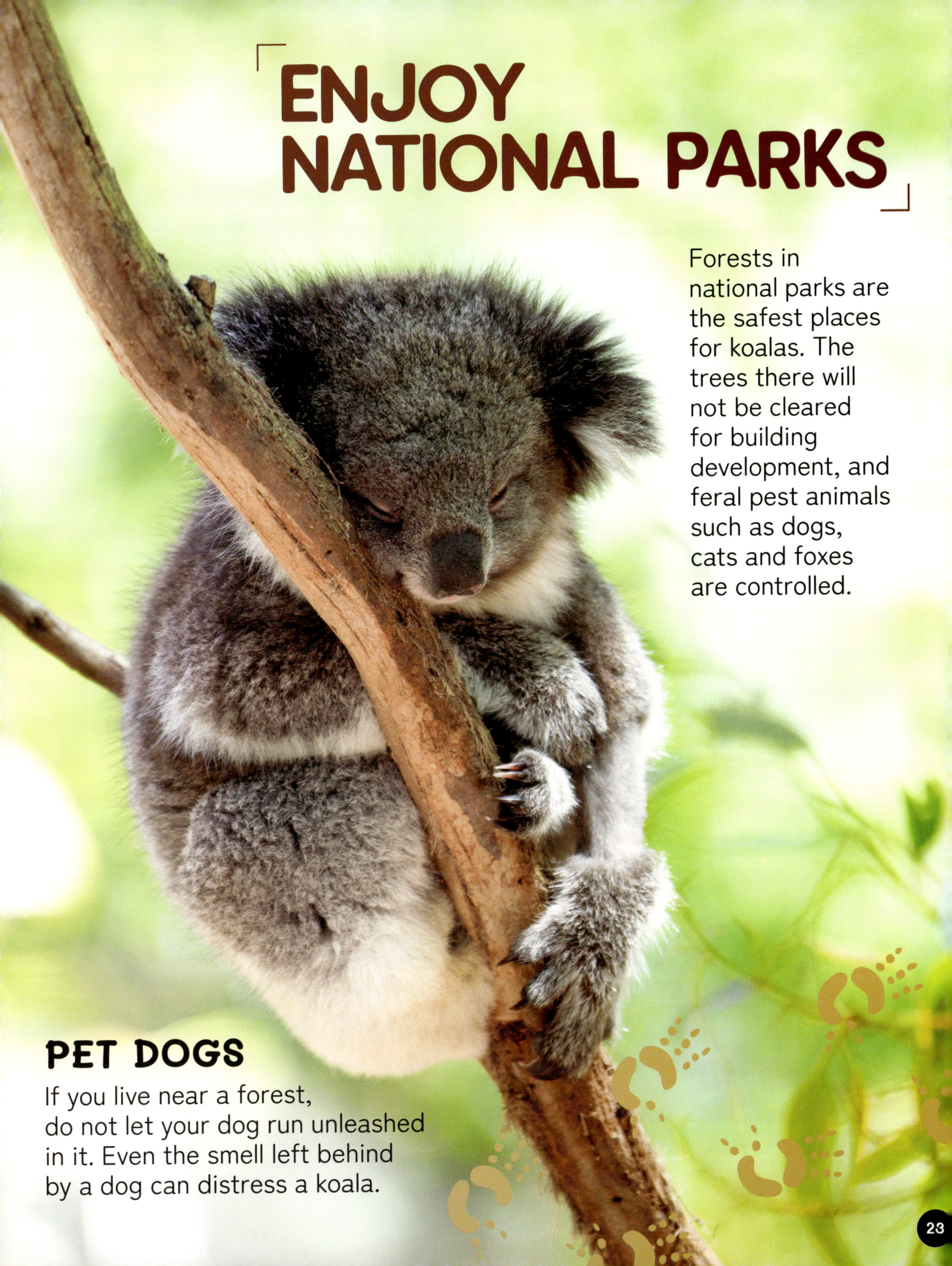

ENJOY NATIONAL PARKS

Forests in national parks are the safest places for koalas. The trees there will not be cleared for building development, and feral pest animals such as dogs, cats and foxes are controlled.

PET DOGS

If you live near a forest, do not let your dog run unleashed in it. Even the smell left behind by a dog can distress a koala.

THREATS TO KOALAS

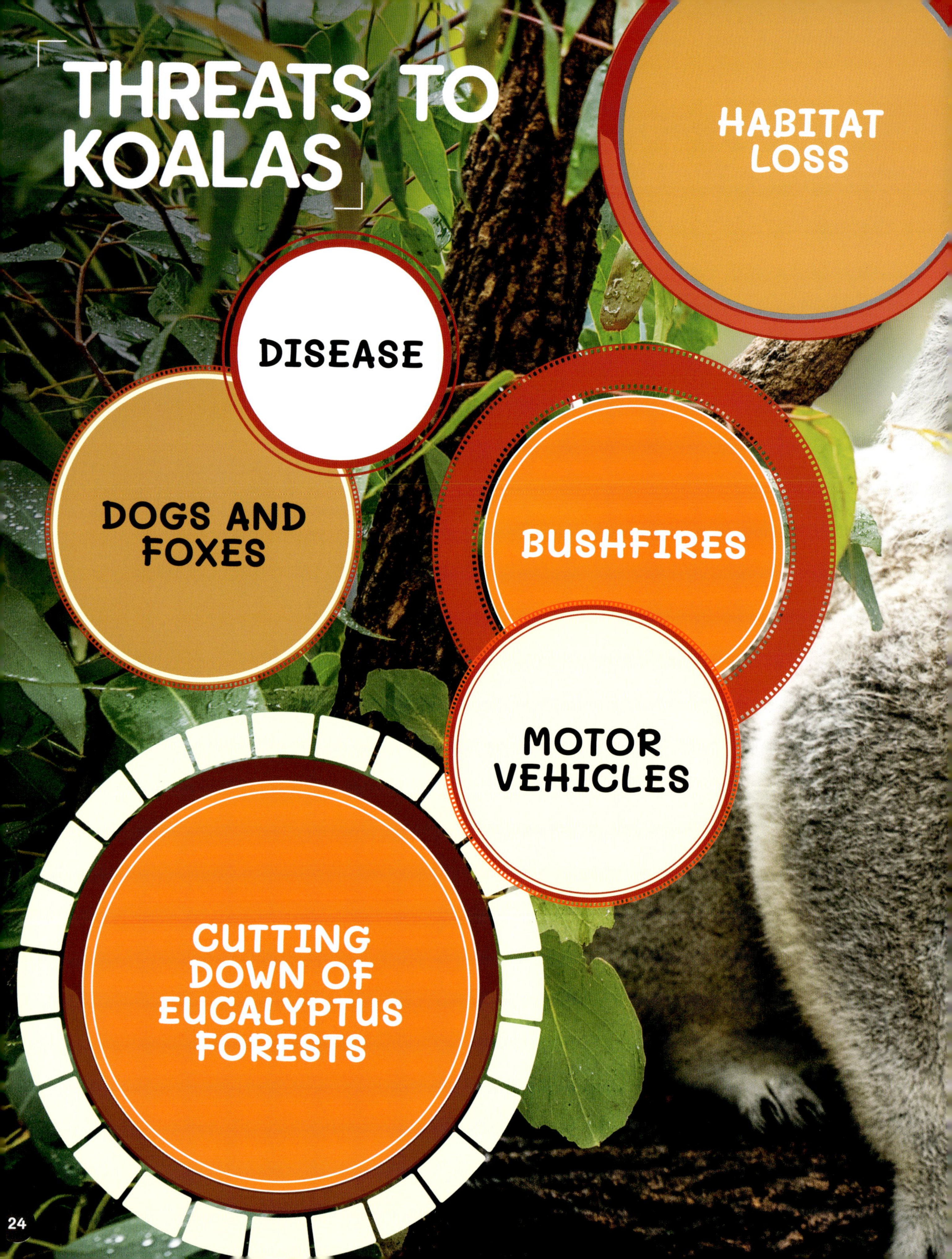

HUNTED FOR THEIR FUR

Up until the early 1900s, koalas were killed for their fur. Millions of skins were exported to make clothing. Although this horrifies us today, it was once common to kill all sorts of Australian animals so their skins could be used for coats and hats. Koala skins were even made into toys for children.

Today, anyone who harms a koala will face very severe legal penalties.

THE FUTURE OF KOALAS

The limited diet of koalas makes them very vulnerable. Anything that destroys the eucalyptus forests will result in the loss of koalas as well.

As more and more people demand housing and places to work, the forests that koalas need will be replaced by buildings.

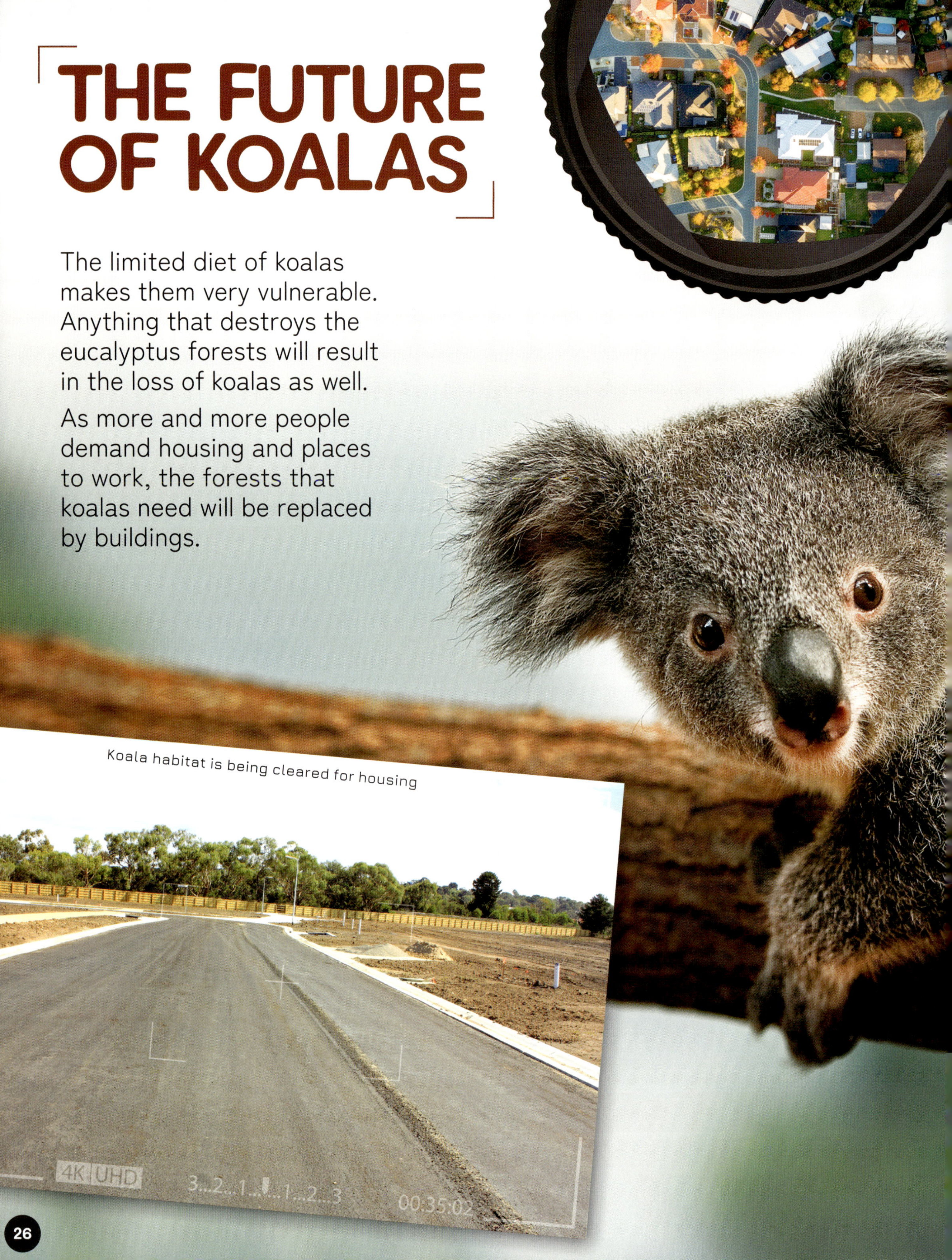

Koala habitat is being cleared for housing

National parks are the only places where koalas are safe from habitat loss, but maintaining or increasing the numbers of koalas in the wild depends on them having enough room to expand their territories.

Having too many koalas in a small area can create problems, including starvation. Since koalas are territorial, moving large numbers of them to small areas, such as on islands, severely disrupts their normal social behaviour and their breeding.

The more we know about koalas, the more we can all help to make the right decisions about the things that will affect them. Research by biologists is one way that we can find out what needs to be done to ensure the future of koalas is a positive one. Will you be one of those biologists?

SORTING ANIMALS INTO GROUPS

Biologists divide all living things around the world into groups. They call this process classification.

Here are the basic groups that describe all animals with backbones:

AMPHIBIANS

Examples include frogs and salamanders. Amphibians start life in water but later grow lungs so they can breathe air on land.

MAMMALS

Examples include dingoes and possums. Mammals are warm-blooded, have fur and feed their young on milk.

FISH

Examples include sharks and goldfish.

BIRDS

Examples include emus and penguins. Birds are the only animals with feathers.

REPTILES

Examples include lizards and snakes. Reptiles are cold-blooded and are covered in scales.

Mammals are further divided into three main groups:

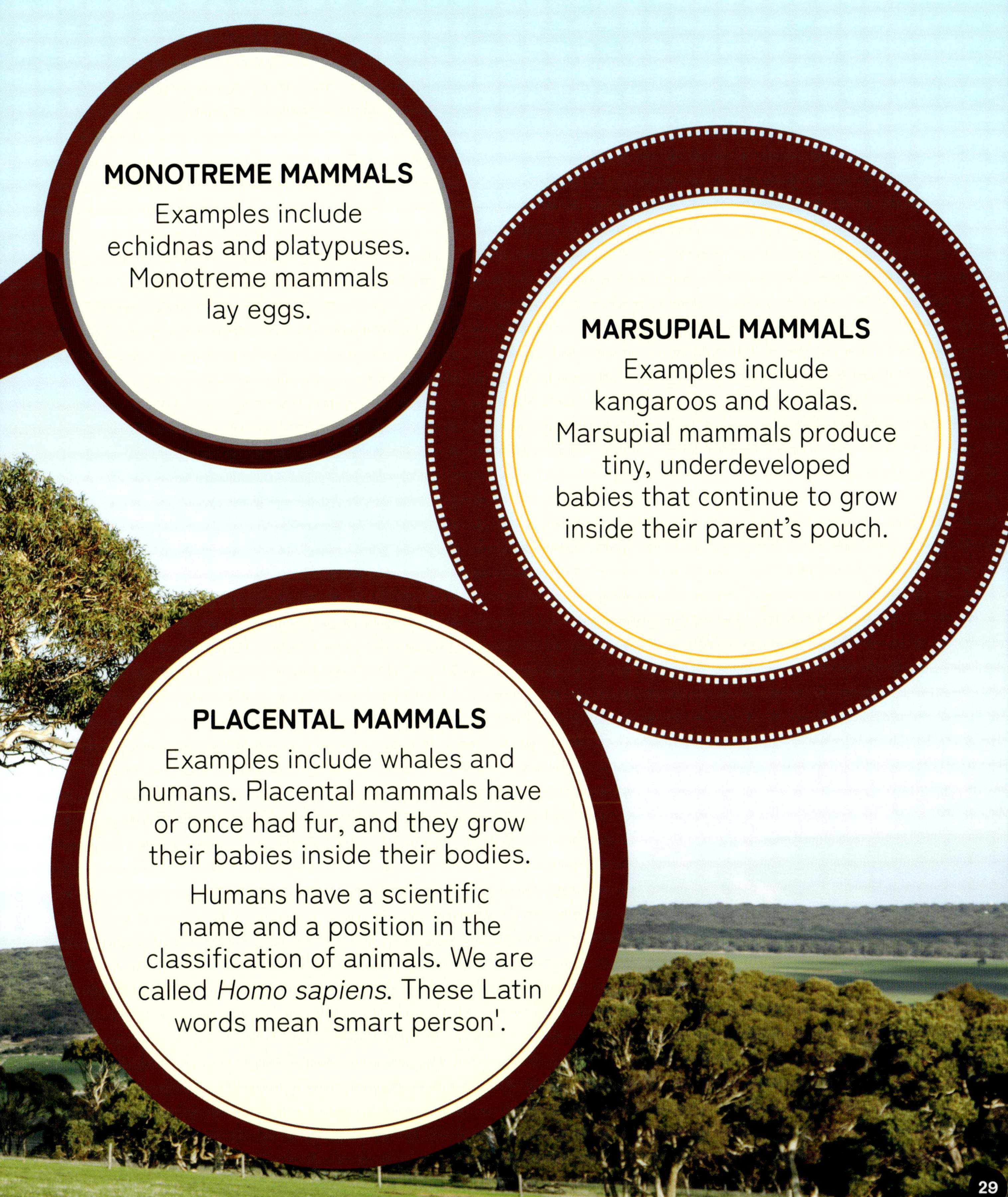

MONOTREME MAMMALS

Examples include echidnas and platypuses. Monotreme mammals lay eggs.

MARSUPIAL MAMMALS

Examples include kangaroos and koalas. Marsupial mammals produce tiny, underdeveloped babies that continue to grow inside their parent's pouch.

PLACENTAL MAMMALS

Examples include whales and humans. Placental mammals have or once had fur, and they grow their babies inside their bodies.

Humans have a scientific name and a position in the classification of animals. We are called *Homo sapiens*. These Latin words mean 'smart person'.

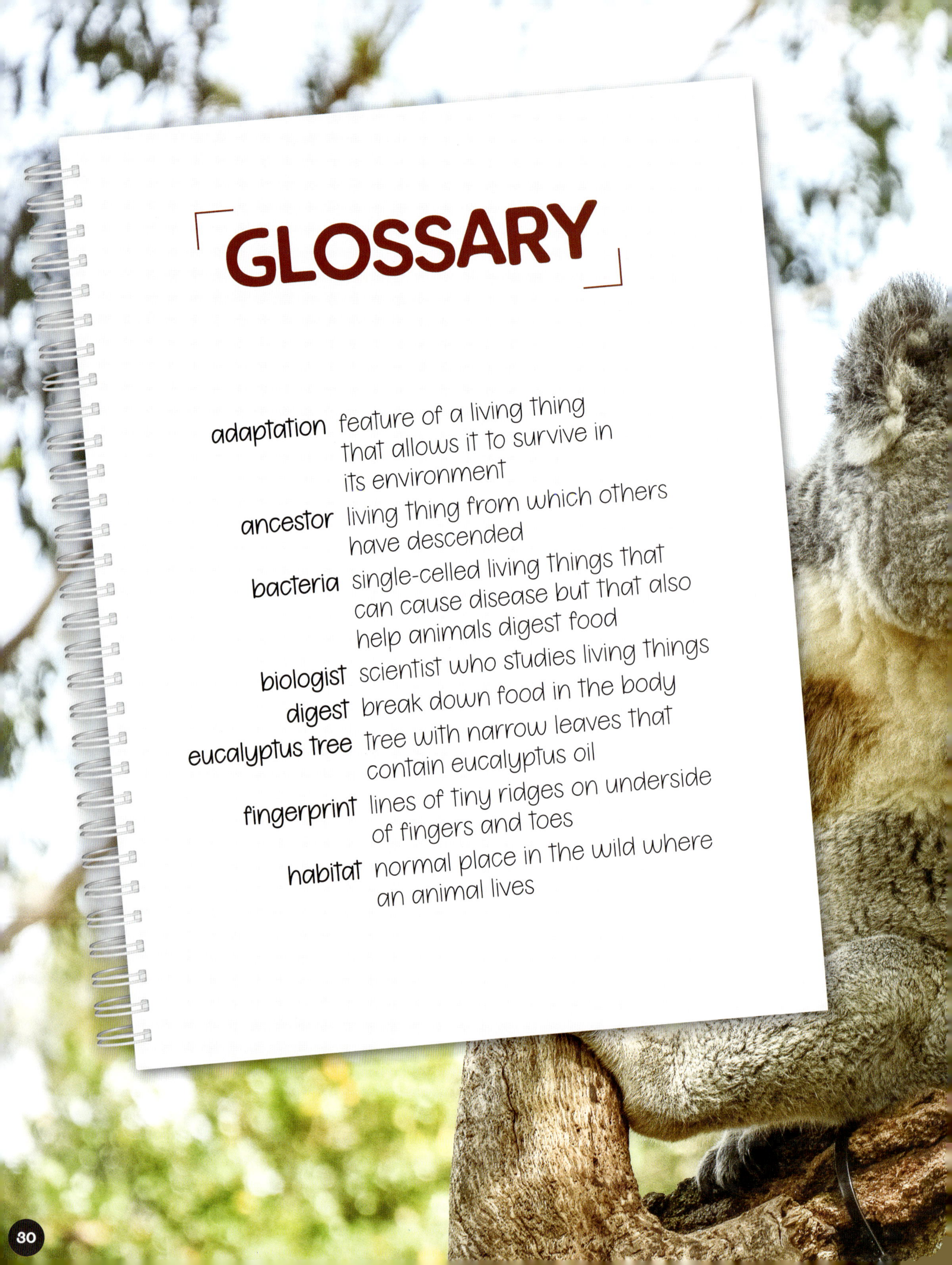

GLOSSARY

adaptation feature of a living thing that allows it to survive in its environment

ancestor living thing from which others have descended

bacteria single-celled living things that can cause disease but that also help animals digest food

biologist scientist who studies living things

digest break down food in the body

eucalyptus tree tree with narrow leaves that contain eucalyptus oil

fingerprint lines of tiny ridges on underside of fingers and toes

habitat normal place in the wild where an animal lives

joey baby marsupial

Latin language used by the ancient Romans and still used for some scientific purposes

mammal animal with fur and that feeds its babies with milk

marsupial type of mammal with a pouch for its babies

pap dark green eucalyptus jelly-like excretion

Phascolarctos cinereus Latin words that mean 'grey bear with a pouch'

rainforest dense forest in warm, high rainfall area

territory area that an animal claims for itself to live in

vulnerable under threat

INDEX